MOSES AND THE GREAT ESCAPE

Bible Bedtime Story

BLUME POTTER

INTRODUCTION

In the quiet moments before bedtime, as the day winds down and little ones prepare to drift off to sleep, there's a unique opportunity to fill their minds with stories that inspire, teach, and comfort. Moses and the Great Escape is more than just a collection of Bible stories—it's a journey of faith, courage, and the enduring power of God's love, tailor-made for the curious hearts of children.

This book brings to life one of the most dramatic and impactful stories in the Bible, making it accessible and engaging for young readers. Through the eyes of Moses, your children or grandchildren will embark on an adventure that not only entertains but also imparts valuable lessons about trust, bravery, and the importance of following God's guidance.

Each chapter, from the burning bush to the miraculous parting of the Red Sea, is crafted to capture the imagination while gently embedding timeless truths. The simple yet profound narrative style is perfect for bedtime reading, helping to create a peaceful and reflective end to the day.

As grandparents and parents, you have the privilege of guiding the next generation in their spiritual journey. Moses and the Great Escape is a tool that will not only bring joy and excitement to bedtime but also lay a foundation of faith that will stay with your children for a lifetime. Let this book be a cherished addition to your family's bedtime routine, where each night, a new lesson from Moses' extraordinary journey unfolds, nurturing your child's heart and soul.

CHAPTER ONE:
THE BURNING BUSH

Moses was a shepherd, spending his days in the quiet of the desert, tending to his sheep. The sun was high in the sky, and the heat made the air shimmer like water. Moses walked along, guiding his flock to a patch of green grass near the foot of Mount Horeb, also known as the Mountain of God. It was just another ordinary day, or so Moses thought.

As he approached the mountain, something caught his eye. In the distance, a bush was on fire. But there was something strange about it—the bush was burning, but it wasn't being consumed by the flames. The leaves and branches were glowing with fire, yet they remained perfectly intact. Moses had never seen anything like it.

Curiosity got the better of him. He left his sheep grazing and walked closer to the bush. The closer he got, the more incredible the sight became. The flames danced around the branches, but the bush did not burn up. Moses knew he had to get closer to understand what was happening.

When Moses was near enough to touch the bush, a voice called out to him from the flames.

"Moses! Moses!"

Moses froze in his tracks. "Here I am," he replied, his heart pounding in his chest.

"Do not come any closer," the voice said. "Take off your sandals, for the place where you are standing is holy ground."

Moses quickly removed his sandals, realizing that this was no ordinary fire—this was something divine. The voice from the bush continued to speak.

"I am the God of your father, the God of Abraham, the God of Isaac, and the God of Jacob."

Moses hid his face, afraid to look at God. He knew he was in the presence of something far greater than himself.

"I have seen the suffering of my people in Egypt," God said. "I have heard their cries for help because of their harsh treatment as slaves. I know their pain, and I have come down to rescue them from the hand of the Egyptians. I will bring them to a good and spacious land, a land flowing with milk and honey."

Moses listened intently, but he couldn't imagine what any of this had to do with him. He was just a shepherd, far away from the struggles of his people in Egypt.

"And now," God said, "I am sending you to Pharaoh to bring my people, the Israelites, out of Egypt."

Moses was stunned. Him? Lead the Israelites out of Egypt? It seemed impossible. Moses' mind raced with doubt and fear. How could he, a simple shepherd, confront the mighty Pharaoh and lead an entire nation to freedom?

"Who am I, that I should go to Pharaoh and bring the Israelites out of Egypt?" Moses asked, his voice trembling.

God's response was calm and reassuring. "I will be with you. And this will be the sign to you that it is I who have sent you: When you have brought the people out of Egypt, you will worship God on this mountain."

Even with God's promise, Moses felt nervous. But deep down, he knew that if God was with him, anything was possible. Moses took a deep breath and nodded. He didn't understand everything yet, but he knew he had to trust in God's plan.

And so, Moses' extraordinary journey began—not as a powerful leader, but as a humble shepherd, guided by faith and the promise that God would be with him every step of the way.

CHAPTER TWO:
LET MY PEOPLE GO

Moses knew it wouldn't be easy, but with God's promise in his heart, he returned to Egypt. The memories of his past in the palace came flooding back, but now he was there on a different mission—a mission from God. Moses wasn't alone; his brother Aaron was with him, and together, they went to meet Pharaoh, the powerful king of Egypt.

The palace was grand and intimidating, but Moses and Aaron walked with purpose. When they were finally in the presence of Pharaoh, Moses spoke the words God had given him.

"Thus says the Lord, the God of Israel: Let My people go, so that they may worship Me."

Pharaoh looked at Moses with disdain. "Who is the Lord, that I should obey Him and let Israel go? I do not know the Lord, and I will not let Israel go."

Moses repeated God's command, but Pharaoh's heart was hard. He wasn't about to let the Israelites go free—they were his slaves, the backbone of Egypt's labor force. Pharaoh refused, and instead, he made the Israelites' work even harder.

Moses and Aaron were disheartened, but God had warned them that Pharaoh would be stubborn. God then told

Moses that He would send signs and wonders to show Pharaoh His power.

The first sign came when Aaron threw down his staff before Pharaoh, and it turned into a serpent. But Pharaoh's magicians did the same with their own staffs, so Pharaoh wasn't impressed. He hardened his heart and refused to listen.

So, God began to send plagues upon Egypt, each one more severe than the last. First, the waters of the Nile River turned to blood, making it undrinkable and killing the fish. But Pharaoh's heart remained hard.

Next came the plague of frogs. They swarmed over the land, in people's homes, their beds, and even their ovens. Pharaoh pleaded with Moses to ask God to take away the frogs, and he promised to let the people go. But as soon as the frogs were gone, Pharaoh changed his mind.

Then came a plague of gnats, followed by a swarm of flies. The air buzzed with insects, causing misery throughout the land. But still, Pharaoh's heart was stubborn.

God sent a disease that killed the Egyptians' livestock, but Pharaoh's heart did not soften. Then, painful boils broke out on the skin of the Egyptians, but still, Pharaoh would not let the Israelites go.

Hail rained down from the sky, destroying crops and homes, followed by a swarm of locusts that devoured anything left in the fields. Pharaoh begged Moses to ask God to stop the plagues, but once they were gone, Pharaoh hardened his heart again.

Finally, darkness covered the land of Egypt for three days—thick, impenetrable darkness. But Pharaoh's heart remained as hard as stone.

God had one last plague, the most severe of all. He warned Pharaoh that every firstborn in Egypt would die if he did not let the Israelites go. But even this warning did not move Pharaoh's heart.

And so, the night came when the final plague struck Egypt. The firstborn in every Egyptian household, from the son of Pharaoh to the lowliest servant, died. The cries of grief echoed through the land.

It was only then, in the face of such great loss, that Pharaoh finally relented. His heart was broken, and he called for Moses and Aaron in the dead of night.

"Go," Pharaoh said, his voice heavy with sorrow. "Leave my people, you and the Israelites! Go, worship the Lord as you have requested. Take your flocks and herds, and be gone. And bless me also."

Moses and Aaron wasted no time. They gathered the Israelites, and together, they prepared to leave Egypt. The time of their captivity was over, and they were about to embark on a journey to freedom, guided by the hand of God.

CHAPTER THREE:
THE ESCAPE FROM EGYPT

The night of the final plague had shaken Egypt to its core. As the first light of dawn appeared, the Israelites, led by Moses, prepared to leave the land where they had lived in slavery for generations. There was no time to waste; Pharaoh had finally allowed them to go, but Moses knew that they needed to move quickly.

Families hurriedly packed their belongings—what little they could carry. Mothers gathered their children, fathers loaded up donkeys, and everyone prepared to leave behind the only home they had ever known. The air was filled with a mixture of excitement and fear. They were finally free, but the road ahead was uncertain.

Moses led the way, his staff in hand, guiding the people towards freedom. The Israelites moved as one, a massive throng of people stretching out as far as the eye could see. Their destination was the land that God had promised them, a place where they could live in peace and worship Him freely.

But as they journeyed away from Egypt, news reached Pharaoh that the Israelites had left. The grief of losing his firstborn son still weighed heavily on his heart, but now anger and pride took over. Pharaoh changed his mind once again. How could he let his slaves go? Who would build his cities and tend to his fields?

Pharaoh called for his army, the best chariots, and his most skilled soldiers. "We must bring them back!" he commanded. The Egyptians quickly prepared for battle, determined to chase down the Israelites and force them to return to Egypt.

As the Israelites approached the Red Sea, they began to hear the distant rumble of chariots. Fear spread through the camp like wildfire. They were trapped—the vast sea stretched out before them, and Pharaoh's army was closing in behind them. Panic set in, and the people turned to Moses, their voices filled with fear and desperation.

"Why did you bring us out here to die?" they cried. "It would have been better for us to stay in Egypt as slaves than to die here in the desert!"

Moses stood tall, his faith unwavering. He knew that God had not brought them this far to abandon them now. With a calm but firm voice, he spoke to the people, "Do not be afraid. Stand firm, and you will see the deliverance the Lord will bring you today. The Egyptians you see today, you will never see again. The Lord will fight for you; you need only to be still."

The Israelites quieted down, their eyes fixed on Moses, waiting to see what would happen next. They were trapped between Pharaoh's powerful army and the seemingly impassable Red Sea. But Moses knew that this was no ordinary journey—they were being led by the hand of God, and their path to freedom was about to unfold in a way that none of them could have imagined.

CHAPTER FOUR:
THE MIRACLE OF THE RED SEA

As the Israelites stood at the edge of the Red Sea, with Pharaoh's army closing in, the tension was palpable. But Moses remained calm, trusting in the power of God. He knew that their escape from Egypt was not the end of the story—it was just the beginning of God's mighty plan.

God spoke to Moses, "Raise your staff and stretch out your hand over the sea to divide the water, so that the Israelites can go through the sea on dry ground."

Moses obeyed without hesitation. He lifted his staff high above his head and stretched out his hand over the Red Sea. In that moment, a powerful wind began to blow, and the waters of the sea began to part. The Israelites watched in awe as the water formed towering walls on either side, leaving a dry path straight through the middle of the sea.

"Go!" Moses commanded, and the Israelites, filled with a mixture of wonder and urgency, began to walk across the seabed. Men, women, and children hurried along the path, their eyes wide with amazement. The ground beneath their feet was dry, and the walls of water on either side shimmered in the sunlight. It was a sight none of them would ever forget.

Behind them, Pharaoh's army was relentless. Seeing the path through the sea, they charged forward, determined to capture the Israelites and bring them back to Egypt.

The chariots thundered towards the sea, but God was not finished with His miracle.

As the last of the Israelites set foot on the opposite shore, Moses once again lifted his staff over the sea. With a mighty rush, the walls of water collapsed, and the sea returned to its full depth. The powerful waves crashed down, engulfing Pharaoh's army in an instant. The chariots, horses, and soldiers were swept away, unable to pursue the Israelites any further.

On the other side of the sea, the Israelites stood in silence, staring back at the vast waters that had just saved them from certain capture. The danger was gone, and they were free—truly free at last.

Moses lowered his staff, and the people erupted in cheers of joy and gratitude. They had witnessed a miracle, and they knew that God was with them. He had delivered them from the hands of their enemies, just as He had promised. The journey to freedom was far from over, but the Israelites were filled with hope and faith, knowing that God was guiding them every step of the way.

CHAPTER FIVE:
A JOURNEY OF FAITH

The Israelites stood on the far shore of the Red Sea, their hearts filled with gratitude and awe. They were free—no longer slaves in Egypt, but a people set on a journey toward a land that God had promised them. Their voices rose in joyful songs of praise, thanking God for His miraculous rescue and for Moses, who had led them to safety.

But the journey was far from over. The path to the Promised Land led through a vast and barren desert, a place of uncertainty and challenge. Moses knew that the road ahead would not be easy, but he trusted in God's guidance, and he encouraged the people to do the same.

As they traveled, the Israelites faced many difficulties. The desert was hot and dry, and soon they began to worry about food and water. But God had not brought them this far to abandon them. Each time they faced a need, God provided. When they were hungry, He sent down manna from heaven, a bread-like substance that appeared on the ground each morning. When they were thirsty, God instructed Moses to strike a rock, and water flowed out, enough for everyone to drink.

Despite these miracles, the Israelites sometimes doubted and complained. They missed the comforts of Egypt, even though they had been slaves there. But each time they grew weary or fearful, Moses reminded them of God's faithfulness. He encouraged them to keep their eyes on the Promised Land and to trust that God was with them every step of the way.

As they journeyed through the desert, God led them by a pillar of cloud during the day and a pillar of fire by night, showing them the way to go. The people of Israel learned that they could depend on God, not just for their physical needs, but for guidance, protection, and strength.

The journey through the desert was long, but it was also a time of growth. The Israelites were learning what it meant to be God's chosen people, to live by faith, and to trust in His promises. With each step, they moved closer to the land that God had set aside for them, a land flowing with milk and honey, where they would finally find rest.

And so, the journey of faith continued, with Moses leading the way, guided by the hand of God. The Israelites had much to learn, but they knew that they were not alone.

God was with them, providing for their every need, and leading them towards a future filled with hope and blessing.

www.ingramcontent.com/pod-product-compliance
Lightning Source LLC
Chambersburg PA
CBHW081204130726
47996CB00009B/3241